Seasonal Activities
Autumn & Winter
Caroline Matusiak

Bright Ideas
for Early Years

Published by Scholastic Publications Ltd,
Villiers House, Clarendon Avenue,
Leamington Spa, Warwickshire
CV32 5PR

© 1991 Scholastic Publications

Written by Caroline Matusiak
Edited by Janet Fisher
Sub-edited by Catherine Baker
Designed by Sue Limb
Illustrations by Mary Lonsdale
Photographs by John Twinning (p.5),
Dennis Mansell (p.9), Bob Bray (p.10),
Richard Butchins (pp.29, 41), Mrs K.
Stevens (p.49), Lorna Minton (p.50), Terri
(p.63), Caroline Matusiak (pp.75, 89).
Cover by Martyn Chillmaid
Jacket on front cover loaned by Adams
Childrenswear.

Artwork by Liz Preece,
Castle Graphics, Kenilworth
Printed in Great Britain by
Loxley Brothers Ltd, Sheffield

The publishers wish to thank Pitman
Publishing for permission to quote 'Here
is a tree with its leaves so green', and
Evans Brothers Ltd for permission to
quote 'Four scarlet berries'.

British Library Cataloguing in Publication Data
Matusiak, Caroline
    Bright ideas for early years: seasonal activities, autumn/
    winter.
    1. Primary schools. Activities
    I. Title
    372.'1332

ISBN 0-590-76507-8

Contents

For Thomas Anthony

Introduction

The seasons provide a wealth of material for early learning. Seasonal changes in nature, weather and temperature are reflected in the clothes we wear and what we do, and so provide abundant opportunities for experience and activities that are the essence of early childhood education.

Changes in the world around them are a constant source of fascination for young children. Each day brings such discoveries as fruits that fall and snow that freezes, and with these, new possibilities of seeds to plant and gloves to wear. Staff can follow children's interests and heighten their awareness of seasonal changes, making the most of the potential of the various topics to provide a balanced curriculum. In exploring the richness of the seasons, staff can share children's wonder and delight.

Seasonal topics

The seasons lend themselves easily to topics. For example, 'Leaves' seems a natural topic in autumn, and 'Toys' in winter, which is the traditional time for exchanging presents. Topic work with very young children needs to be based on their direct experience and interests. Seasonal topics are useful in this respect, offering materials, experiences and activities that are part of children's everyday life. However, there is also the opportunity to develop children's awareness and extend their knowledge of the world around by providing related activities and close observation over a period of time.

The everyday activities and experiences of children form the basis of their curriculum. All areas of learning, including the core subjects, English, maths and science, are woven into the fabric of these experiences and provide the foundation for future knowledge.

Technology provides an approach and an application for many subject-based concepts. Teachers, informed of the subject areas, are able to interpret and extend young children's experiences. The following subject guide gives a brief indication of how these areas of learning can be enhanced for young children.

English

Speaking and listening form an integral part of all areas of learning. As young children learn, they strive to name and express ideas of increasing complexity, and sharing activities and experiences involves them in communicating with others. New ideas are often expressed in words with which children are already familiar: 'It sticks,' said Becky, when she put the magnet on a biscuit tin. Children are actively using and adapting language to fit their purposes, drawing on known structures and usage.

A teacher's role lies in encouraging language development, by listening to children and giving them the opportunity to talk about what they are doing. Teachers provide a model of language use, offering new words and structures that children can assimilate and build on. The 'Talk about' section of each activity suggests ideas for developing language across the curriculum.

Reading and writing develop within a literacy environment, where children are encouraged to behave like readers and writers, demonstrate their knowledge and simultaneously practise new skills. Topics provide a source of material for wall rhymes, role play and the writing centre which will encourage writing and reading for a purpose. Ideas for motivating reading and writing habits are not confined to one topic. The wall rhyme suggested in 'Autumn leaves' can equally well be used in another topic.

Maths

Teachers who are aware of the maths potential of everyday activities can foster children's understanding and experience. Topics based on the seasons can provide a meaningful way of extending these activities.

Children gain familiarity with number names and sequence as they sing number rhymes with seasonal themes. One-to-one correspondence is practised in a meaningful way when children use their fingers to represent the objects in the song. Surveys of favourite fruit bring the opportunity to record number for a purpose.

Shape and space are explored when natural objects are used for printing and making impressions, introducing three and two dimensions. The girths of tree trunks are compared using non-standard measures. Food activities provide an enjoyable means of introducing standard measures and time.

The attributes of natural and man-made objects can be named and sorted according to different criteria. The seasons bring a variety of natural events and objects to observe, discuss and record.

Science

The changing seasons offer a wealth of science activities which help children to become aware of the variety of life, the weather, and the range of different materials and their uses. These are part of children's everyday life, and the opportunity to observe them at first hand, using all five senses, lies literally at the doorstep. Nurture a responsible attitude to the environment by collecting wildlife and plants sparingly, caring for them appropriately and returning them to their original habitat. Check with parents for any fur or feather allergies.

Food activities are a good source of science work relating to seasonal change, and offer scope for observing the effects of heating and cooling, and looking at substances in different forms. They are also tasty! It is important to remember hygiene where food is concerned. Before carrying out any food activities with children, check with parents for any food allergies.

Children are naturally curious, wanting to investigate, explore and predict outcomes. With increasing experience, they begin to think and talk in the abstract, hypothesising and reasoning.

Technology

Each season brings new opportunities to look at machines that are part of our lives, and to consider how they are used. Young children's natural tendency to pull things apart and see how they work can be encouraged, and alongside it the motivation to design and construct. Children's willingness to solve problems and plan materials can be nurtured with your support.

Finding out

Provide reference books to support each topic. These should be available in many areas of the nursery — for example, in the book corner alongside favourite story books, or on the investigation table to support the materials presented there. You can also put books about houses and vehicles in the construction area, and recipe books with pictures of meals from all over the world in the food area.

At story time, read some suitable non-fiction with the children as well as stories, so that they become familiar with the format and language patterns of both reference and story books.

When teachers or children need further information about a topic, there is a perfect opportunity to use reference books for a purpose. Every chance can be taken to help the children to use books to find the answers they need.

About the activities

Each topic contains activities of the following two types:
- 'Let's discover . . .' and 'Let's look for . . .'. These activities suggest ideas for relevant investigation tables, where children can actively participate in collecting, arranging and labelling examples.
- 'Let's meet . . .' and 'Let's visit . . .'. These activities suggest ideas to enable children to observe English, maths, science and technology in context.

Reading, writing and the application of maths are made purposeful when children participate. Exploring the natural and man-made environment leads to children's own discoveries and questions. At the same time, children can explore the local area and meet people at work. Experience of places and people gives an impetus to children's role play when they imitate people and create characters and use literacy and maths for a purpose.

About the topics

Each seasonal topic offers a range of experiences in most curriculum areas. The subject components are included to show that activities undertaken in the nursery are the foundation for later education. However, the early years' curriculum is founded on the social, emotional, physical and intellectual development of children. These remain as important as ever.

A secure child is ready to explore and experiment, a sociable child is willing to communicate with others, and overall physical development ensures that children handle equipment effectively. The topics suggested in this book provide scope for promoting these fundamental aims. The topics and activities are intended as ideas for teachers to adapt and incorporate according to the needs and interests of their children. Above all, the ideas presented here are intended to be enjoyable.

Autumn

Autumn is associated with leaves changing colour and falling, and with the harvest of grain, fruit and vegetables. Leaves can be studied as a source of food and as a home for insects. Fruit and vegetables offer a wealth of colour, shape and tastes to explore. Eating bread is familiar to most young children, but the making of bread with flour and yeast may not be.

When visiting the park with the children and walking around the school grounds, photograph the children and the things they see. The photographs will help to start a seasonal diary, recording the natural and man-made environment, as well as the clothes children wear at different times of the year. Start a year book by taking photographs of school visits and visitors. This helps children to remember and sequence events.

The topics for this season are 'Leaves', 'Fruit and vegetables' and 'Bread'.

Leaves

Chapter one

Falling leaves are a sign of autumn. A visit to the park gives children a chance to observe trees and leaves. Printing with leaves lets children look closely at their shape, while all five senses can be used in studying the leaves we eat. A close investigation of some different leaves can be fascinating for the children. Their discoveries of insects on leaves will introduce the idea of a leaf as a home. Creating a habitat for a stick insect provides a subject for close observation, as well as an introduction to camouflage.

The children may wonder what happens to leaves on the ground and in the street. Setting up a wormery and a visit from a refuse collector will explain nature's and man's solutions.

Let's visit the park

Objectives

Science: observing the variety of trees and leaves, and investigating seasonal changes.

What to do

Take the children for a walk around the park, looking at trees and plants. What shape are their leaves? What colour are they? Ask the children to look at leaves that are changing colour, and to examine the leaves of conifers and other evergreens such as holly. Are all the trees losing their leaves? Collect fallen leaves from several trees and plants. Are they the same or different? What animals, birds and insects make their home in a tree?

Ask the children who is in the park. What are they doing? Perhaps there are gardeners, children playing on the swings and people out for a walk. Ask the children what *they* like to do in the park. With adequate supervision, children can use the park facilities to feed ducks, play ball, have a swing and picnic in fine weather.

Follow-up
English

Retell the events in the park in sequence as a group, encouraging as many children as possible to participate. It is interesting to discover the incidents and features that are memorable to children. A picnic often proves to be the highlight.
Maths

Encourage the children to use their bodies to explore shape and movement. Ask them to run and turn, bending and stretching as they represent leaves whirling in the wind, and then to stand or lie still in a leaf shape. Turn this into a game. When the music plays, they should move like leaves in the wind; when it stops, they should stand motionless.

Let's discover leaves

Objective
Science: observing the variety of leaves.

What you need
A selection of leaves, plants with leaves, such as chrysanthemum, lavender and geranium, and small branches from hedges and trees.

What to do
When selecting leaves include variegated specimens, such as those on a spider plant, and silvery-grey ones such as pyretheum. Succulents provide an interesting variation and are easy to propagate, especially the varieties that produce new plants around the edge of each leaf. However, if cacti are to be introduced, take care to ensure that children cannot touch them as some cacti, particularly opuntias, have needles that are painful and difficult to remove. Cacti can be observed inside an empty minibeast tank with a lid.

With the children's help, set the plants out on the investigation table. Provide a magnifying glass for close observation. Encourage the children to take care of the plants, watering them as required.

Talk about
Leaves: their size, shape, number, colour, smell and texture.

Follow-up
English
Make a wall chart in the shape of a leaf or plant, on which children who have watered the plants can write their names.
Science
Help the children to propagate some succulents. A leaf or section planted in sandy soil quickly takes root. They can propagate spider plants by pegging the new plants into the pot while they are still attached to the parent plant. The new

plants can be detached when they start to produce new leaves.

Sorting leaves

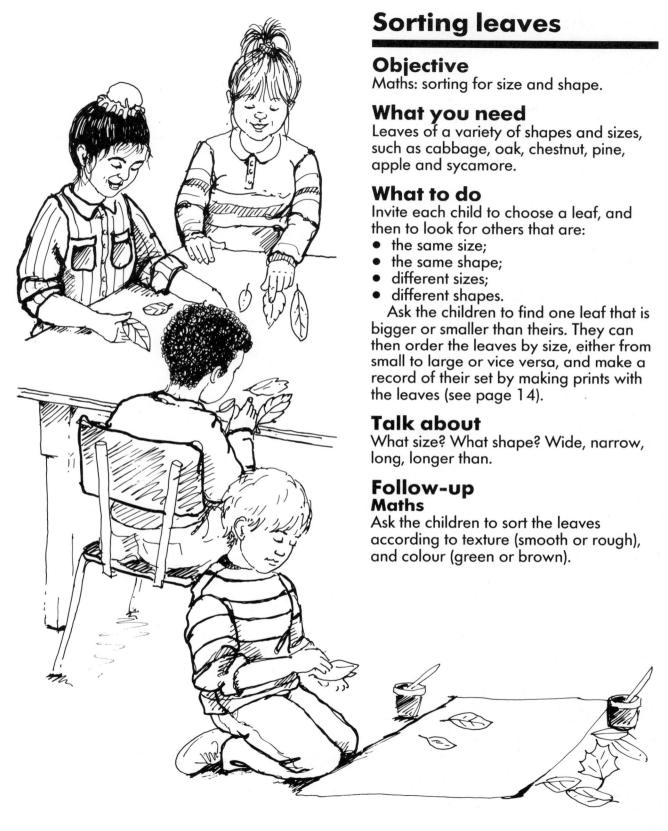

Objective
Maths: sorting for size and shape.

What you need
Leaves of a variety of shapes and sizes, such as cabbage, oak, chestnut, pine, apple and sycamore.

What to do
Invite each child to choose a leaf, and then to look for others that are:
* the same size;
* the same shape;
* different sizes;
* different shapes.

Ask the children to find one leaf that is bigger or smaller than theirs. They can then order the leaves by size, either from small to large or vice versa, and make a record of their set by making prints with the leaves (see page 14).

Talk about
What size? What shape? Wide, narrow, long, longer than.

Follow-up
Maths
Ask the children to sort the leaves according to texture (smooth or rough), and colour (green or brown).

Printing with leaves

Objectives
Maths: investigating three-dimensional and two-dimensional shapes, and looking at pattern.

What you need
Trays of thick ready-mixed paint, a piece of sponge soaked in paint to help avoid drips and provide an even coat, leaves of different sizes and shapes, paper.

What to do
Ask the children to press a leaf on to the paint-soaked sponge and then to press the leaf on to the paper. They should then turn the leaf over and repeat the activity. Provide a choice of leaves and colours.

Talk about
What shape? The patterns of the leaf veins.

Follow-up
Maths
● Cover large sheets of paper with leaf prints. Try using the back of untreated wallpaper, or plain wallpaper with a raised surface. These can be used for a background to children's paintings or for an autumn frieze. They also provide an effective wallpaper for the home corner.
● Provide twigs, cones and grasses for printing.

Leaf rubbings

Objective
Science and maths: observing pattern in nature.

What you need
Thin paper such as newsprint, chunky wax crayons, an assortment of leaves.

What to do
Ask each child to place a leaf under a piece of paper. Using the side of the crayon they should rub over the paper on top of the leaf. Both sides of the leaf can be used in this way. Ask the children to compare the wax rubbings. They can then choose another leaf and repeat the activity.

Talk about
Parts of a leaf: stalk, veins, leaflet.

Follow-up
Science
Show the children how to make bark rubbings, using logs or trees. Compare the barks of different trees. Masking tape can be used to secure paper to the trunk. Encourage the children to make rubbings on a cross-section of a log or tree that has been felled, and look at the pattern and spacing of the rings. Explain what the rings signify. How many rings are there? How old is the tree?

Sewing leaves

Objective
Maths: using mathematical language.

What you need
A variety of leaves, open-weave material such as binca or the netting from vegetable sacks, wool in autumn shades, for example, brown, orange and yellow, large blunt needles, scissors.

What to do
Using a real leaf as a template, cut leaf shapes from the fabric with the children's help. Thread the needles with wool, tying a knot at the needle end to prevent the wool from unthreading when it is pulled through the fabric.

Invite the children to choose a leaf shape and some wool. Encourage them to devise their own way of decorating the leaves with stitches. Some may sew around the edges, while others may try crossing stitches of different colours. The opportunity to explore thread is more important than producing a row of neat stitches, and any large uneven stitches will appear attractive on this leaf design.

Talk about
On top, underneath, the edge, long and short stitches, cross.

Box of leaves

Objective
Science: observing seasonal changes in living things.

What you need
A box, a variety of leaves.

What to do
Ask the children to collect leaves which are still green. Put the leaves in the box. Encourage the children to handle the leaves and look at them carefully. Observe and discuss the changes daily as the leaves become crisp and crackly when handled.

Talk about
Firm, glossy, green, withered, dried, crackly, brown, yellow.

Follow-up
Science
Take the children for a walk through leaves under a tree. Ask them to listen to the swishing sound as their feet walk through the newly-fallen leaves. Later, return to listen to the crackle of dried leaves.

Falling leaves

Objective
Science: observing seasonal changes in living things.

What you need
A vase or container, twigs from different trees (both deciduous and evergreen) with green leaves attached, water.

What to do
Fill the vase with water and put in the twigs. Encourage the children to observe the changes over several days. They should compare the deciduous leaves with the evergreen ones.

Talk about
Tree names, leaf texture, shape and colour, deciduous and evergreen.

Follow-up
Science
Take the children out to observe trees in the grounds or nearby. Discuss whether the trees are losing their leaves.

Autumn leaves

Objective
English: encouraging familiarity with print and practising reading behaviour.

What you need
Card or paper, thick felt-tipped pens in different colours.

What to do
Choose one of the children's favourite rhymes, or use the example given here. Write down the words using rebus, pictures instead of words, at key points. Give colour clues by using a felt-tipped pen of the appropriate shade. Use different styles of print for onomatopoeic words such as swishing, crackling and crunching. This makes these words easy to identify as the children recite the rhyme, helping to keep the match between the spoken and the written word.

Let the children watch, and ask them to recite the rhyme as you write it down. Point out to them the left to right direction of print as you write and when you read. Answer any questions they may ask about writing.

Read the rhyme with the children, pointing out the words with your finger. Ask the children to read it to you. Stick the rhyme on a wall at the children's height. Children can return and repeat the rhyme on other occasions.

Red autumn (leaves)
Lying on the ground.
Pick (l) up
It's (l) I've found.
Listen to their swishing sound
crunching crackling
All around.

Autumn leaves

Red autumn leaves
Lying on the ground.
Pick one up
It's **one** I've found.
Listen to their swishing sound,
Crunching, crackling all around.

Brown autumn leaves
Lying on the ground.
Pick one up
It's **two** I've found.
Listen to their swishing sound,
Crunching, crackling all around.

Yellow autumn leaves . . . etc
It's **three** I've found.
Listen to . . . etc.

Orange autumn leaves . . . etc
It's **four** I've found.
Listen to . . . etc.

Green autumn leaves . . . etc
It's **five** I've found.
Listen to . . . etc.

Caroline Matusiak

Talk about
Writing, letters, spaces, words, words of the rhyme, adding on one, number names, colours and sounds.

Follow-up
Maths
Count five leaves or fingers when saying the rhyme. When reciting 'Autumn leaves', the children add on one each time. Many familiar rhymes such as 'Five little buns' (see page 47) involve taking away one.
Science
Use real leaves, and ask the children to look at their colours and name them. Alternatively, paint five leaves in the five autumn colours and invite the children to choose and name the colour of leaf for each verse.

A wormery

Objective
Science: observing the variety of life.

What you need
A plastic tank, dark-coloured paper, soil, sand, leaves, some worms.

What to do
Place layers of moist sand and soil in the tank. On top of this place the leaves and worms. Cover the sides of the tank with dark paper. After a few days the activity of the worms will be visible.

Children enjoy hunting for worms outside, but they should be encouraged to take care when digging out and handling worms. It is easier to find worms when they come to the surface after a rain shower. Ensure that worms are returned to their habitat after observation.

Talk about
Worm shape, movement, dark, tunnels, decaying leaves.

Follow-up
Science
Ask the children to observe what happens to dead leaves on the street and in the playground. With the children's help, sweep up some leaves from the playground and start a compost heap that can be spread on the flower-beds in the spring.

Let's meet the refuse collector

Objective
Science: observing that human activities produce waste products.

What to do
Arrange for a refuse collector and dust-cart to visit during school hours. Before the visit, consider items that are thrown away in the classroom, such as paper, broken toys and milk cartons.

Ask the children how paper is made. Why are things thrown away? Where do they go?

Trace the route of a milk carton: its arrival at school in the morning on the milk van, its function at milk time, and then how it finds its way to the school bin via the classroom bin.

Sweep up leaves and litter from the nursery grounds into a bag and await the arrival of the dust-cart. Watch as the school rubbish and the class bag is loaded.

Talk about
The work of the refuse collectors, driver, loader, the parts of the vehicle. Where the rubbish goes. Trees, paper, wood.

Follow-up
Science
Discuss ways of using rubbish. Make a compost heap for garden waste, and save packaging for junk-modelling and plastic containers for growing seedlings.

Leaves we eat

Objective
Science: investigating leaves using sight, touch and taste.

What you need
A cabbage or a lettuce, a knife.

What to do
Let the children hold the cabbage and feel its weight. Look at the way in which the leaves encircle the centre.

Ask the children to pull off a leaf, and trace the path of the leaf's veins with a finger. Invite them to pull off some more leaves and see how closely they fit together.

Cut the cabbage in half. Show the children the layers of the leaves with the stalk running through the middle. See how tightly packed the central leaves are. The children should compare the smooth stalk with the rough texture of the outside leaves.

Ask the children to smell the cabbage. Break off some more leaves and shred or tear them into strips. Let the children taste them.

Talk about
What can you see, smell, touch and taste?

Follow-up
Science
Boil a cabbage in water. Discuss with the children how it has changed in texture and taste.

Coleslaw

Objective
Science: observing with all five senses.

What you need
Half of a white cabbage, half of a red cabbage, three carrots, three apples, a grater, a knife, a bowl.

What to do
Grate or finely shred the cabbages and carrots. Chop the apples. Let the children mix them together in a bowl. Ask them to taste the mixture.

Talk about
Colour, taste and smell, chop, grate, shred, mix.

Herbs

Objective
Science: observing with all five senses.

What you need
A selection of fresh herbs such as dill, thyme, marjoram, parsley and mint. These can be bought in large supermarkets, or grown from seed in the nursery garden or in pots inside the classroom.

What to do
Ask the children to look at and compare the different leaves. Let them smell each one. Herbs can be tasted, but young children rarely like their sharp flavour. It would therefore be better to add them to food as appropriate; for example, a pizza (see page 44).

NB Tell the children not to eat leaves and berries that they may find elsewhere.

Talk about
Herb names; the texture and smell of herbs.

Follow-up
Science
Dry a selection of herbs by tying the stalks together with string and hanging them upside down. These can be used in a pot-pourri for the classroom.

Autumn impressions

Objective
Maths: observing pattern and shape.

What you need
Clay, a clay cutter, a pointed clay tool or an old pencil, a variety of leaves, cones, acorns, sycamore wings, twigs, other natural materials.

What to do
Using a clay cutter, slice the clay into slabs about two centimetres thick. Give a slab of clay to each child and let him press a leaf firmly into the clay. The leaf should then be carefully peeled off.

Let the children choose another leaf and repeat the activity. The children can write their names on the clay using a thin twig or clay tool.

Using the clay tool, make a hole at the top of each slab. Leave the impressions to dry out. The slabs can then be hung up for display.

Talk about
Impression, press, pattern, shapes.

Follow-up
Maths
Provide twigs, leaves, cones and grasses in the wet sand tray and on the dough table, and encourage the children to make impressions with them.

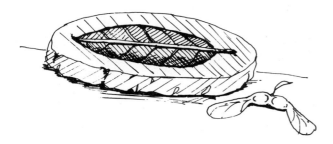

Autumn collage

Objective
Maths: using space and shape.

What you need
Strong paper or firm fabric such as hessian, adhesive, natural materials such as leaves, straw, wood shavings, twigs and grasses.

What to do
Ask the children to choose a natural object, apply adhesive and press it on to the paper or fabric backing. Ask them to make a pattern or picture with the materials. Brush adhesive over the leaves to preserve them.

Talk about
What shape? Object names, covers, does not cover, fit together.

Follow-up
Science
Ask the children to fill shakers with parts of a tree such as nuts, nutshells, seeds, bark and wood. Let them listen to the different sounds. Use the instruments to accompany 'Autumn leaves' on pages 18 and 19.

Autumn water tray

Objective
Science: observing floating and sinking.

What you need
A water tray, natural materials such as cones, bark, twigs, a small log, conkers, leaves, a potato, a carrot.

What to do
Ask the children to predict whether the materials will float or sink. Place the materials one at a time in the water tray and discuss the results.

Leave the materials in the water tray to form part of the children's imaginative play.

Talk about
Floats, sinks, on the surface, below the surface.

Follow-up
Maths
To record the results of the experiment, place the objects that float and those that sink on separate trays. Mark each tray with an illustrative label.

Stick insects

Objectives
Science: observing the variety of life and investigating the conditions necessary to sustain insect life.

What you need
Stick insects, their food (for example, privet leaves), a container filled with water for the leaves, a minibeast tank covered with fine netting.

What to do
Before introducing the stick insects, discuss with the children any insects that they may have found on leaves during previous activities. Do the children know where the insects live? What do they eat? Encourage the children to see the similarity between the stick insect and the twigs of privet on which it lives. Ask them to look after the insect and to gather fresh twigs regularly and keep the tank clear of old food.

Talk about
Insects: what do they look like? What do they eat? Where do they live?

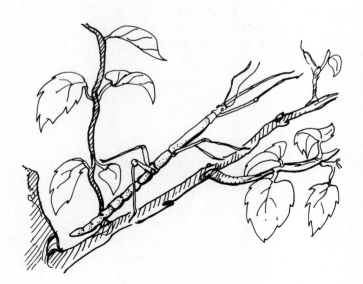

Planting bulbs

Objective
Science: observing the growth of roots and leaves.

What you need
Bulbs such as hyacinth and crocus, a bowl, compost, a transparent bulb holder or plastic bottle cut to fit a bulb, water, dark coloured paper, a newspaper.

What to do
Place one bulb, such as a large hyacinth bulb, on the transparent bulb holder filled with water. The water should be up to the bulb to encourage root growth, but not touching it to prevent rotting. Plant more bulbs in a bowl filled with compost. Water and cover these bulbs with dark paper.

Let the children see that first the roots emerge from the bulb, and then the leaves appear. This is, of course, particularly evident in the transparent container, but you can partially uncover the roots of the bulbs in the bowl of compost for a short time.

When the plants finally turn to seed, remove them from their containers and place them on newspaper, side by side. Encourage the children to observe and handle the plants, exploring the root systems.

You can plant more bulbs in the nursery garden. Children particularly enjoy seeing the snowdrops they planted appear when everything else seems dead.

Talk about
Parts of a plant: bulb, stem, roots, leaves, flower, seeds.

Follow-up
Science
Make a collection of tree leaves and their seeds, such as horse-chestnuts and sycamore wings. These seeds can be grown, but they take several months to germinate (see page 37). However, they often grow where they are not required in gardens and grounds, and these seedlings can be planted in a tub and brought into the nursery for the children to watch as the leaves appear. The plants can later be replanted at a site where they will be able to grow to maturity.

Let's look for orange

Objective
Maths and science: sorting and matching for colour.

What you need
Natural and man-made objects that are orange coloured. Seasonal ideas include chrysanthemums and leaves; other ideas are oranges, a hazard beacon, a protective jacket and a goldfish.

What to do
Let the children look at all the different orange objects, and talk about the varying shades of the colour that they can see.

Discuss with the children the reasons why people might choose to colour something orange — so that it can be clearly seen, perhaps. Link this with orange berries and flowers, whose bright colours attract birds and bees.

Talk about
Orange, names of objects and their functions.

Follow-up
Science
Let the children mix yellow and red paints to make shades of orange.

Tree trunks

Objective
Maths: measuring for size.

What you need
Long strips of thin card, a stapler.

What to do
Ask the children to choose two trees, a mature tree and a younger one. Let them walk around each tree. How many footsteps does it take?

Take a strip of card and hold it round one of the trees. Mark or cut the length of card and then remove it from the tree. Fasten the two ends of the card together with a stapler to make a circle that has the same circumference as the tree trunk. Repeat this with the other tree.

Let the children compare the sizes of the two circles of card. Can one or more children fit inside the large circle? Does the smaller circle fit over someone's wrist or head?

Talk about
Measure, smaller than, larger than, how many?

Follow-up
Maths
Show the children how to measure their wrists, waists and heads with strips of card. Cut the card to size. The children can then use the headbands to make hats, the wristbands to make bracelets or watches and the waistbands to make belts.

Let's look for wood

Objective
Science: observing the types and uses of materials.

What you need
Sawdust of different grades, logs, twigs, planks, sandpaper, wooden objects.

What to do
Place on a table some wood off-cuts (without splinters) and some sandpaper for the children to use to smooth and shape the wood. Collect some everyday articles made from wood, for example, pencils, rulers, building bricks and paintbrushes. Include an old wooden artefact, perhaps a toy or a household implement. Do the children know whether this article is still made from wood? If not, which material is used today?

Talk about
Wood, its colour and texture. Sawdust, logs, planks, sanded, polished.

Follow-up
Maths
Let the children build with wooden bricks, feel their smooth surfaces and sort them into shapes such as cylinders and cuboids. Can they see how the faces fit together? Let them try balancing and tessellating wooden bricks. Compare these with plastic construction materials such as LEGO and Mobilo.

Science
Ask the children to look for wood in the classroom, for example, window sills. Outside the classroom, they could spot wooden fences. Encourage them to listen to and use wooden musical instruments.

Technology
Help the children to design and make models using wood off-cuts. Demonstrate how wood can be sawn to different lengths and joined with nails or adhesive. Let them use tools that are used for woodwork, for example, a screwdriver and a hand drill.

Fruit and vegetables

Chapter two

A supermarket visit presents children with a vast display of fresh, frozen, canned and preserved vegetables and fruit. In the nursery, the fruit and vegetables can be classified, perhaps according to their colour and texture. Fruit seeds can be planted and their growth charted.

When studying different fruits and vegetables children can use all of their senses. The activities suggested involve different ways of preparation including squeezing for juice, chopping and applying heat. Young children are also given an opportunity to use their knowledge of number and writing to record their favourite fruit.

Let's visit the supermarket

Objectives
English: using writing to aid memory.
Maths: measuring for weight and the function of money.
Science: observing the variety of fruits and vegetables.

What to do
Arrange to visit a supermarket with the children. Before the visit, write shopping lists together and refer to them while shopping.

Visit the fruit and vegetable counter. Ask the children to look at and name the fruits and vegetables. Interest them in the colours; the yellow bananas, grapefruit, sweetcorn and lemons; the green apples, lettuces, limes and grapes.

Let the children select some fruit and vegetables. They can feel the weight of them in the basket. Let them weigh the goods on the customer scales. Ask the children to hand over the goods to be weighed and priced by an assistant.

Visit the canned and frozen food sections. Do the children know what fruit or vegetable is in each tin or packet? Look at the jams and jellies. Which jam or jelly flavour do they prefer? Look at fruit juices and squash. How many fruits can they recognise? Buy a selection of the above for tasting.

Talk about
Fruit and vegetable names, colours, shapes, flavours, heavy, light.

Follow-up
English
Rearrange the home corner to make a supermarket. Include pads and pencils for shopping lists, as well as brochures and hand-outs to encourage literacy. Provide real potatoes and a balance for weighing.

ORANGES

BANANAS

Let's discover fruit and vegetables

Objective
Science: observing the variety of fruit and vegetables.

What you need
Fresh and tinned fruit and vegetables, jam, empty fruit and vegetable packets, recipe books, food pamphlets.

What to do
Arrange a selection of fresh and tinned fruit and vegetables and jam on a table. Invite children to search through the scrap materials and look for containers that held fruit in different forms: fruit juice packets, plastic squash bottles, jelly packets and other foods that include fruit flavour, such as yoghurt and mousse. Empty frozen fruit and vegetable packages often have colourful pictures of the product. Recipe books and pamphlets from local stores are also useful for showing different fruit and vegetables.

Talk about
Names of fruit and vegetables, how they are preserved.

Sorting fruit and vegetables

Objective
Maths and science: sorting and classifying into broad groups according to different criteria.

What you need
An assortment of fruit and vegetables, possibly those which are to be used in the soup and fruit salad activities on pages 34 and 36.

What to do
Ask the children to separate the fruit from the vegetables. Then ask them to sort them by criteria such as colour and shape. Next, they can group together those with leaves, those that grow under the ground, those that are peeled and those containing seeds or stones.

Talk about
Colour, shape, the same, different, belongs, does not belong.

Vegetable prints

Objective
Maths: exploring shape.

What you need
Two carrots, a potato with an interesting shape, half a turnip that has been hollowed out (these may well be the remains of the soup, see page 34), paint, a thin piece of sponge, shallow dishes, paper.

What to do
Cut one carrot in half lengthways and the other in thick rings. Slice the potato in half through the interesting part.

Mix some thick paint for printing. Soak the paint into a thin sponge for even printing. Let the children press the vegetable shapes on to the sponge and then on the paper to create a variety of prints.

Talk about
Shape, section, rings, smaller, larger, print, same shape.

Follow-up
Maths
Slice a few potatoes in half and carve a simple pattern on each surface. Let the children print with them. They could try printing on smooth and rough surfaces.

Tops and tails

Objective
Science: observing that certain conditions help sustain life.

What you need
Old potatoes that are ready to sprout, carrot or turnip tops.

What to do
Leave the potatoes to grow roots. Ask the children to watch how the potato shrivels as the roots get longer.

Place the carrot or turnip tops in water and tell the children to look out for new leaves.

Talk about
Vegetables that grow under the ground, roots and their function.

Follow-up
Maths
Get the children to estimate which of the potatoes has the longest root. They could measure the roots using lengths of different coloured wool for each root. Ask the children to compare the lengths of the wool and roots.

Raw vegetables

Objective
Science: observing a variety of
vegetables, using all five senses.

What you need
Celery, a carrot, an onion (all preferably
with leaves and roots still attached), a
knife.

What to do
Ask the children to look closely at each
vegetable in turn. They should examine
the leaves and roots of the carrot.
Discuss which parts of the plant grow
under the ground. Look at the roots and
talk about their function in feeding the
growing carrot plant. Look for any
bumps or indents. Point out that these
were probably formed in stony soil. Ask
the children whether any of their pets like
to eat carrots.

Look at the celery. Examine the leaves
and root. Encourage the children to look
at the wide celery sticks on the outside
and the narrower ones in the centre.
Open the celery gently to look for the
newest and smallest stick.

Look at the onion. Show the children
the roots that are still evident and, if
possible, look at the onion stalks. Open
the onion and examine its layers of peel,
including the brown outer layer, the
yellow skin and the white inner layers.
Point out how these follow the shape of
the onion.

With the children, clean and prepare
the vegetables. Cut the carrot and celery
into sticks and dice the onion finely. Offer
them to the children to smell and taste if
they wish.

Talk about
Vegetable names, raw, parts of the
vegetable, their smell and taste.

Follow-up
Science
Cook the vegetables and ask the children
how they have changed in texture and
taste. A palatable way of achieving this
is by making soup; see page 34.

Carrot cake

Objective
Science: observing the effects of heat.

What you need
125g self-raising wholemeal flour, half a teaspoon of mixed spice, 100ml sunflower or vegetable oil, 125g brown sugar, two eggs, 175g finely grated carrot, 50g raisins (optional), greaseproof paper, a cake or loaf tin, a wooden spoon, a whisk, an oven.

What to do
Involve the children as much as possible in this activity.

Mix the flour and spice in a bowl. Whisk the eggs and brown sugar until thick and creamy. Whisk the oil slowly into the egg mixture. Stir in the flour and spice, and then the grated carrot. Add raisins, if required.

Spoon the mixture evenly into a cake or loaf tin that has been greased and lined. Bake at 190°C, 375°F or gas mark 5 for about 30 minutes until firm. Slice and serve when cool.

Ask the children what differences they can see in the cake before and after baking.

Talk about
Carrot, grate, dry ingredients, sugar, grease, line a tin.

Soup

Objective
Science: observing changes caused by applying heat.

What you need
A selection of vegetables including celery, leek or onion, potatoes, turnip, carrots, with baby corn and green beans for colour and interest, herbs to taste, a set of plastic spoons and containers such as margarine tubs for tasting, a knife, a large spoon, a transparent saucepan, water, a cooker.

What to do
With the children's help, clean and prepare the vegetables, noting the texture and colour. Put some raw vegetables aside to use for comparison later. Dice the rest finely and add water. At a safe distance, the children can watch as the water boils and then simmers. Ask them to watch the movement of the vegetables in the boiling water. Cook until soft and serve when the soup is warm but not hot. Remind the children to look for pieces of the carrot and other vegetables and ask them to compare their texture and taste with the raw vegetables.

Talk about
Vegetable names and parts, raw, cooked, boiling, hard, soft.

The enormous turnip

Objective
English: listening to traditional tales.

What you need
An enjoyable story with a simple plot —
the tale of the enormous turnip is suitable.

What to do
Choose a story which you enjoy, and
which you feel will appeal to the children.

A story-telling session can gain in
immediacy if you tell the tale without
using a book. Rather than trying to
remember the whole story word for
word, divide it into sections:
1. Introducing the old man and his wife.
2. The sowing of the seed.
3. The growth of the turnip.
4. Pulling the turnip up.

The first time round, keep the
characters and story simple. However,
familiarity brings confidence, and you will
soon start embellishing the characters
and adding extra details to your
description of events.

Some tips: Keep the descriptions
simple, but include some realistic snippets,
for example, 'he pulled until his back
ached'. When you know that children
have had real experience of certain
incidents, refer to them in more detail, for
example, in describing the making of
turnip soup (see page 34) and its inviting
smell.

Use facial expressions and gestures to
support your words. Simple but effective
props, such as a large turnip, can help
enhance the story.

Talk about
Story terms such as, 'There was once',
and 'A long time ago'.

Follow-up
English
Leave one of the story's props in the role
play area and observe the children's
play. Using felt, cut out the characters in
the story. Leave these in the book corner
for children to practise telling stories to
each other.
Maths
Encourage the children to explore shape
and space by acting out the story in the
school hall. They could curl up small to
represent the seed, use their arms and
legs to show the roots and shoots,
experiment with ways of showing how
the turnip grows bigger, and mime
digging up the turnip with a spade.

Fruit salad

Objective
Science: observing a variety of fruit, using all five senses.

What you need
Two apples, two pears, two bananas, less familiar fruit such as kiwi fruit, a carton of unsweetened fruit juice, a knife, a large bowl, a small bowl and spoon for each child.

What to do
Ask the children to look carefully at the fruit, noting its colour, shape and texture. As the fruit is cleaned and prepared, get them to look for its seeds. Retain the seeds, comparing their size, colour and shape.

If blunt children's table knives are available, the children can help in cutting soft fruit such as the pears and bananas. Put the prepared fruit into a bowl. Add fruit juice from the carton and serve.

Help the children to identify the different fruits using taste, colour and texture.

Talk about
Fruit names and parts, texture, colour and shape.

Follow-up
Science
Introduce apples of different colours and varieties to the children and ask them to taste and compare them.

Favourite fruit

Objectives
Maths: recording on a bar chart.
English: making marks.

What you need
A clipboard, a pencil, paper, clear photographs from a magazine or drawings of three different kinds of popular fruit.

What to do
Divide the paper into three columns. Stick or draw a picture of one type of fruit at the top of each column. An older child can conduct a survey, asking each child in turn to write her 'name' under her favourite fruit. It sometimes helps to draw a box for each name.

Display the chart. Count with the children how many people like each fruit. Count how many children took part.

Talk about
How many? More than, less than, the same number, number names.

Fruit juice

Objective
Science: observing changes.

What you need
Oranges, lemons, a juice squeezer, a set of plastic spoons for tasting.

What to do
With the children's help, squeeze the oranges and lemons separately. Ask them to taste and compare the juices.

Talk about
Fruit, juice, pips, peel, rind, segment, stone, sweet, sour.

Follow-up
Science
Get the children to look at packets of fruit juice to see which sorts of fruit are included. Let them taste the juices to see which they like.

Planting seeds

Objective
Science: observing the life-cycle of a tree.

What you need
Apple and pear seeds, possibly from the fruit salad on page 37, some small stones, soil or compost, two plant pots, an indoor cloche.

What to do
Allow the children to help as much as they can.

Soak the apple and pear seeds for a couple of days. Put some small stones at the bottom of each pot, and cover them with soil or compost. Use one pot for pear seeds and the other for apple seeds, planting several seeds in each pot. Water the pots and place them in the cloche.

It often takes several weeks before seeds germinate, but growing trees from fruit seeds fascinates young children. Ask them what they think will happen to the seedlings, and encourage them to look at the pots regularly while the young plants are growing.

Talk about
Fruit, seeds, conditions for growth, moist, warm, rain, sun, seed dispersal.

Follow-up
English
With the children recall and retell the story of the seeds and fruit, including the fruit salad.
Maths
Make a photo sequence book to show what happened to the fruit and seeds, in order to encourage the children to talk about time.

Sharing apples

Objective
Maths: introducing number notation and fractions.

What you need
Apples, a clipboard, paper, a pen, a pencil, a knife.

What to do
Divide the children into small groups, and ask one child from each group to make a mark on the paper for every child who wants to taste an apple.

Young children may devise their own tally system, often a series of single pencil strokes. Older children, familiar with the form of numbers, often use traditional notation, adding on one for each additional child.

Divide the apple according to the final number and share it out for the children to eat.

Talk about
How many? Number names, divide, share, some each.

Apple pie

Objectives

Maths: measuring with non-standard units.
Science: observing changes that occur when heat is applied.

What you need

A pie dish, four cooking apples, two cups of plain flour, 100g margarine, sugar to taste, water, a cup, a tablespoon, a knife, a rolling pin, an oven.

What to do

Give the children the opportunity to do as much as possible. Measure the ingredients using a cup or a tablespoon. Rub the fat with the flour. Add a little water and knead the pastry until it is pliable. Roll it out to cover the dish. Peel and slice the apples, and place them in the dish with the sugar and a little water.

Cover with pastry, and bake in the oven at 180°C, 350°F or gas mark 4. Wait until the pie is cool before giving some to the children to taste.

Talk about

Apple and pastry texture before and after cooking. Hot, cool.

Follow-up
English

Make a pictorial recipe card using coloured felt-tipped pens and encourage the children to follow it when baking.

Here is a tree

Objective
English: speaking and listening.

What to do
Encourage the children to participate in the following rhyme as a group, performing the actions as well as the words.

Here is a tree with its leaves so green,
[Arm straight with fingers for leaves.]
Here are the apples that hang between.
[Clench fists for the apples.]
When the wind blows the apples will fall,
[Rock arm and fingers as though the wind blows the tree.]
Here is a basket to gather them all.
[Hold out arms in a circle.]

Follow-up
English
Invite the children to take turns to recite a favourite rhyme on their own or with friends.

Bread

Chapter three

The harvest of crops is a traditional feature of this season, and bread is part of children's everyday lives. However, the modern loaf, sliced and wrapped in plastic, seems far removed from the grains of wheat which were harvested to make it. Children can make bread using yeast, and this could lead to an exploration of different types of flour and their uses in baking.

A visit to a baker's shop provides the opportunity to look at food made with flour. Setting up a baker's shop in the nursery encourages role play, using flour to make 'loaves' and 'cakes'. The story of the little red hen sequences the changes from seed to wheat, flour and, finally, bread.

Let's visit a baker's shop

Objectives
Science: investigating the use of wheat in food.
Maths: using money in context.

What to do
Arrange to visit a baker's shop with the children when it is not too busy. Some shops bake on the premises and it may be possible to visit the kitchen and look at the ingredients and machinery used for baking.

A good baker's shop will display bread using a variety of different types of flour, such as wholemeal, granary and white. Ask the children to look at the shapes of the bread and find out their names. They can also look at the sizes and shapes of the rolls. Choose and buy some bread to taste in the nursery, perhaps for making 'shape sandwiches' (see page 43).

Discuss with the children some other uses of flour: to make cakes, biscuits, buns, savoury pies, flans and sausage rolls.

Talk about
Types of flour, names of bread shapes, large and small loaf, rolls, money, cost, change.

Let's discover flour

Objective
Science: investigating the types and uses of flour.

What you need
Samples of different types of flour, small containers, a magnifying jar, stalks of cereal crops, paper flour bags, containers and labels from food containing flour.

What to do
Display samples of different flours in the small containers, and place some in a magnifying jar. Ask the children what differences they can see. Wheat, corn and barley stalks can be sheaved together to show how different they are. Place a head of each against contrasting paper for comparison.

Ask the children to search the scrap materials for containers with labels that show cereal products or flour: pasta, cake mixes and breakfast cereals.

Talk about
Flour, grains, stalk, head, barley, wheat, corn, flour, types of flour, wholemeal, granary, white.

Making bread

Objective
Science: observing the effect of heat on different substances.

What you need
700g wholemeal or strong white flour, 25g fresh yeast, 400ml warm water, one dessertspoon sugar, a mixing bowl, a loaf tin, an oven, a tray, a knife, butter.

What to do
Let the children help as much as possible with this activity. Making bread requires a warm temperature to ensure that the yeast is activated, so try to make it in a warm room.

Add the yeast and sugar to half the warm water and mix together. Leave for about ten minutes in a warm place until it becomes frothy. Add this to the flour, with the rest of the water, to make dough.

Knead the dough and leave it to rise. Knead it again. Place it in a tin and leave it to rise again.

Put the dough in an oven at 200°C, 400°F or gas mark 6 for 40 minutes, or until the bread sounds hollow when tapped. Turn it out on to a tray to cool. Slice the loaf, butter it and let the children taste it while it is freshly baked.

Talk about
Yeast, warm, flour, dough, rise.

Shape sandwiches

Objective
Maths: exploring shape.

What you need
A loaf of wholemeal and a loaf of white bread, biscuit cutters of different shapes, some blunt knives for spreading, margarine or butter, a spread such as cheese, jam or honey.

What to do
Encourage the children to spread their own margarine over half a slice of wholemeal and half a slice of white bread. Offer them a choice of filling and a choice of biscuit cutter.

When they have put some spread on the bread, ask them to put the two slices together. They can then cut the sandwich with the biscuit cutter and eat their shape sandwich.

Talk about
Covering an area, enough, not enough, shape names, on top, underneath.

Pizza

Objectives
Science: observing the effects of heat.

What you need
Two flat baking trays, a rolling pin, a large round biscuit cutter, 225g flour, two teaspoons of baking powder, 50g margarine, water, tomato purée, grated cheese, herbs, an oven.

What to do
Give the children the opportunity to help as much as they can.

Rub the margarine into the flour and baking powder. Add the water to make a pliable dough. Knead it and roll it flat.

Using the cutter, make several small pizza shapes. Place them on the baking trays, and spread some tomato purée on each pizza. Cover with grated cheese and sprinkle with herbs.

Place the trays in a hot oven at 220°C, 425°F or gas mark 7 for approximately 10–15 minutes. Serve the pizzas to the children when they have cooled down.

Talk about
Dough, flat, fit, cheese, grate, melt, chop, roll, warm.

Follow-up
Science
The bread dough recipe on page 43 can also be used as a pizza base. Place thinly rolled dough on the baking trays, add toppings and leave to rise in a warm place before cooking in the oven.

For a very quick pizza, toast one side of half a roll or muffin under the grill. Turn and cover with the cheese and tomato topping. Grill to melt the cheese, and serve.

Pasta

Objectives
Maths: looking at shape and size.
Science: observing the effect of heat.

What you need
Pasta of different shapes; spiral, star, shell, spaghetti and lasagne; a transparent pan, water, a cooker, grated cheese.

What to do
Discuss the sizes and shapes of the pasta with the children. Reserve some for comparison later. Boil the rest in the saucepan until it is cooked. At a safe distance, let the children watch the pasta fill the saucepan as it swells. Compare the cooked and the uncooked pasta for size and shape. Let the children taste the cooked pasta. Grated cheese can be added if required.

Talk about
Flour, shape names, opposites, small, large, swells, cold, hot, hard, soft.

Let's make a baker's shop

Objectives
English: acting and talking in role.
Maths: using money in context.

What you need
A home corner or role play area, baking tins, mixing bowls, tea-towels, an empty washing-up liquid bottle, rolling pins, cake cases, aprons, a table or open cupboard for a 'counter', paper bags, a till, money, shopping baskets, purses, model 'buns' and 'bread', play dough (see page 46), empty cake and biscuit boxes.

What to do
After visiting a baker's shop, talk about the kinds of machinery and equipment that were used. Discuss with the children how a baker's shop could be set up in the home corner or role play area. Follow the children's ideas. Rearrange the cooker, table and cupboard to form a kitchen and shop counter. Place aprons, tins and other baking equipment in the kitchen.

Make some play dough without adding colouring (see page 46). This will make the dough more realistic. The salt in the mixture should prevent the children eating it. Place the play dough in the kitchen area to encourage the children to roll pastry, make 'sausage rolls' and 'cakes', and to place them in tins and in the oven. If the home corner has a carpet, it might be better to move it to avoid damage.

Make 'brown loaves' using the appropriate flour, or paint some white dough (see the recipe for modelling dough on page 46).

Set up a till on the counter, together with cake and biscuit boxes and the home-made cakes and biscuits. Put some shopping baskets, purses and coats in the dressing-up box.

Talk about
The baker's shop, the work of the baker, selling, buying, money and associated terms.

Follow-up
English and maths
Make pictorial price lists for goods sold in the shop. Leave a pad and pencil nearby to encourage the children to write shopping lists.

Play dough

Objective
Science: using flour and observing the effects of heat.

What you need
Two cups of flour, one cup of salt, two cups of water, two teaspoons of cream of tartar, two tablespoons of cooking oil, a pan, a cooker, a wooden spoon.

What to do
Make the play dough with the children watching from a safe distance.

Add all the ingredients to the pan. Cook the mixture over a medium heat, stirring continuously to prevent it sticking to the pan and to ensure a smooth dough.

When the mixture comes away from the sides of the pan, remove it from the heat. Turn the dough out on to a heatproof surface and knead the warm dough until it is pliable.

When it has cooled, place the dough on a table for the children to use. Store the dough in an airtight tin. It will keep for about two weeks.

Talk about
The ingredients, mixing, stirring, heat, liquid, solid, smooth.

Follow-up
Science
Let the children mix some food colourings to make orange or purple, and add varying quantities of colour to the dough to give different shades. Invite the children to choose the colour for the dough.

Dough for modelling

Objectives
Maths: making shapes.
Science: using flour and observing the effect of heat.

What you need
450g self-raising flour, 450g salt, water as required, an oven, paints, paintbrushes.

What to do
Mix together the flour and salt. Add the water to make a pliable dough. Discuss with the children the food they want to sell in their baker's shop, and let them shape the dough into 'biscuits', 'cakes', 'sausage rolls' and 'loaves of bread'. Place the models in a low oven at 130°C, 250°F or gas mark ½ until hard. When the shapes have cooled, encourage the children to paint them in the appropriate colours and leave them to dry. They are now ready for putting in the baker's shop.

Talk about
Flour, oven, heat, soft, hard, shapes.

Five little buns

Objective
Maths: introducing number and number operations.

What you need
Five play dough 'buns' (see page 46).

What to do
Place the 'buns' on a 'counter', perhaps in the home corner baker's shop. With the children, sing the following rhyme:

Five little buns in a baker's shop,
Small and round with sugar on the top.
Along came a girl [boy] called [child's name] one day,
Bought a little bun and took it away.

Invite one of the children to 'buy' a bun. Count the four remaining buns together. Repeat the rhyme starting with 'Four little buns', and continue until there are none left.

Talk about
How many? Number names, take away, less than, none.

Follow-up
Maths
Make a collection of play dough buns of different shapes, for example, square, triangle, circle, star and oblong. As the children take it in turns to choose a 'bun' to take away, ask them to name the shape.
Science
Paint the buns in different colours. This time ask the children to name the colour when they sing the rhyme.

Breakfast cereal

Objective
Maths: making a bar chart.

What you need
A variety of empty cereal boxes, a clipboard, paper, coloured self-adhesive paper.

What to do
Stick the cereal boxes in a row along the top of the sheet of paper. Cut the adhesive paper into strips. Give the children one each. Ask them to stick their strip of paper under the cereal they like to eat for breakfast.

Together, count how many children like each cereal. Compare the results and decide which cereal is the most popular.

Talk about
How many? Number names, more than, less than.

Follow-up
English
Ask the children to write their 'names' on their strip of paper before sticking them on the chart.
Maths
Write the numerals on the strips of paper when counting, to help children relate the number name with the numeral.

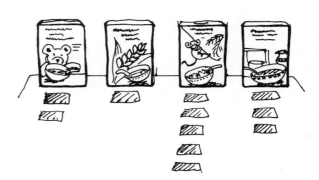

The little red hen

Objectives
English: participating in a story.
Maths: introducing location and direction.

What you need
Children's artwork, including printing and collage based on the autumn activities in this book, pieces of sponge, paint, paper.

What to do
With the children's help, make a frieze based on the story of the little red hen. Mark out a clear route from the farmyard to the field, past the mill and to the baker's shop. The hen's footprints, printed with shapes cut from sponge, will show the route taken.

Talk about
Which way? Where is the . . .? Next to, in front of, behind, to the left, round the corner.

Let's look for brown

Objective
Maths and science: sorting and matching for colour.

What you need
Natural and man-made materials that are brown, for example, soil, grass, leaves, twigs, logs, potatoes, onions, chestnuts, hazelnuts, conkers, brown bread.

What to do
Let the children look closely at all the brown objects. Discuss with them why leaves turn brown in autumn, and how bread and cakes go brown during cooking.

Talk about
Names of brown things.

Follow-up
Science
Take the children for a walk to look for brown items in nature: soil, tree trunks, birds and insects.

Winter

Winter brings shorter days, and young children can experience the contrast between day and night. Children will arrive and leave school in the dark, and safety on the roads becomes an important issue. The weather grows colder, and children need more clothes to keep warm, especially in the snow. The days of ice and snow are fun for children, but they are a threat to the birds. Feeding the birds at this time of year is a valuable experience for the children, helping to develop a sense of responsibility towards wildlife.

At the darkest part of winter, streets are full of lights and activity. Shop windows are bright with toys and gifts, and children's thoughts turn towards wrapping parcels and sending cards. The topics for this season are 'Day and night', 'Keeping warm' and 'Toys'.

49

Day and night

Chapter four

The daily routine takes on a different aspect when children have to get up and go to bed in the dark. Activities associated with day and night each have a distinct identity, and the time of day helps children to differentiate and sequence them.

Shorter days bring dark evenings, and lights are used at home and school. Children can investigate light from different sources, including candles and electricity, while the shadows cast by the winter sun can be the focus of shadow games and activities.

Safety and visibility on the roads are vital at this time of year. The children can investigate colours that can be seen in the dark.

Day and night

Objective
Maths: sequencing daily activities.

What you need
Photographs of the children's daily routine: getting up, having breakfast, arriving at nursery, activities, afternoon play, tea, bedtime; a photograph album or sheets of card.

What to do
Mount the photographs in an album or scrap-book. Alternatively, mount them on individual sheets of card and let the children sequence them. It is easier for the children to do this if the photographs feature only one child.

Talk about
Time, getting up, day, night, breakfast, lunch, tea, bedtime, morning, afternoon, evening.

Follow-up
English
Write captions for the photographs and read them to the children. Place them in the book corner to encourage reading habits.

Goodnight!

Objective
English: speaking and listening in imaginative play.

What you need
A home corner, items connected with bedtime such as a dressing gown, a story book, a teddy bear.

What to do
Add a blanket, a teddy bear, a story book, an old dressing gown, slippers, a towel and other night-time props to the home corner so that children can imitate the sequence of the day by 'going to bed' and 'getting up'. Ensure that the home corner baby has a variety of clothes suitable for night and day which the children can sort.

Talk about
Opposites, daytime, night-time, time to get up, time for bed, asleep, awake.

This is the way . . .

Objective
Maths: ordering activities in time sequence.

What to do
Adapt the well-known rhyme 'Here we go round the mulberry bush' to provide a sequence of day- and night-time activities, starting with verses such as 'This is the way we jump out of bed', '. . . clean our teeth', '. . . eat our breakfast', '. . . walk to nursery', and so on. Include as many references to daily activities as you wish, until the song finishes with, 'This is the way we go to sleep'. Encourage the children to perform the actions associated with the words as they sing them.

Follow-up
Maths
To help settle new children into the sequence of nursery activities, introduce the nursery's daily routine in song and actions: 'This is the way we take off our coats', '. . . paint a picture', '. . . drink our milk', and so on. Ask the children to make up new lines that reflect their favourite activities.

Let's meet a hamster

Objectives
Science: looking at the variety of life and investigating animals that are awake at night.

What you need
A pet hamster in a cage.

What to do
Arrange for a pet hamster to visit the nursery. Leave the hamster in his cage on a table so that the children can watch him.

Ask the owner to feed the hamster. Get the children to look closely at the food and try to identify different types of seed.

Do the children know how the hamster exercises? Discuss how the hamster sleeps during the day and wakes at night. You will be unlikely to demonstrate this as it would be very unusual for any hamster to remain asleep in the nursery!

Discuss with the children any other pets they may have that are awake at night, for example, cats. Do the children know why some animals are awake at night? What do they do? Where do they go?

Talk about
Hamster, its features, colour, habits, food, night, day, light, dark, awake, asleep, seen, not seen.

In the dark

Objective
Science: exploring light and vision.

What you need
A large box with a lid, some small toys.

What to do
Invite a child to choose and place some small toys inside the box. Put the lid on.

Make a small hole in the side of the box. Ask another child to look through the hole and name the toys in the box. What colour are the toys? Can they be seen clearly?

Remove the lid and ask the child to look at the toys again. Does she know why the toys can be seen better now? Listen carefully to the children as they start to reason, question and offer explanations for what they experience.

Repeat the activity with a different child or group of children hiding and looking at the toys.

Talk about
Light, dark, no light, see, not see. Why? Because.

Let's meet the lollipop person

Objective
Science: investigating colours that show up in the dark.

What you need
A visit from a lollipop person dressed for duty.

What to do
Invite a lollipop person to talk about his or her work and to advise on how children can cross the road safely.

Ask the children to look at the clothes that the lollipop person wears. Do they know what colours they are? Why are those colours worn?

Ask them to look at the 'lollipop'. Do they know what it means to drivers? Discuss the lights that are switched on to warn traffic of a hazard ahead.

Talk about
Road safety, dark evenings, being seen, traffic lights, street lamps, crossing with the lollipop person.

Keeping safe

Objectives
Maths: understanding shape and measuring with non-standard units.
Technology: designing and making.

What you need
Fluorescent self-adhesive paper, scissors, pencils, lengths of ribbon or string for measuring.

What to do
Ask the children to choose whether they would rather make a fluorescent badge or a strip to wear on their coat. Those who want to make badges can draw a freehand shape on the fluorescent paper and cut around it.

Before making a strip, children need to decide where they are going to wear it. It could be on their back, around a sleeve or across one side of their coat. Encourage the children to measure the chosen place with string, use the string to measure out the right length of paper and cut the strip. Stick the strip on the coat as planned.

NB Fluorescent badges and strips are useful, but reflective ones that beam back a car's headlights to the driver are more effective.

Talk about
What sort of? Shape, size. How long? Fits, longer, shorter, too long, too short, road safety.

Electric light

Objective
Science: investigating electricity and safety.

What you need
A 3.5 volt bulb, a bulb holder, four paper clips, a flat 4.5 volt battery, two wires with stripped ends.

What to do
While the children watch, make a simple electrical circuit in the following way.

Fit a paper clip to each of the terminals of the bulb holder and to each of the contact tabs of the battery. Attach one end of each wire to a paper clip on the battery and the other end to a paper clip on the bulb holder in order to light the bulb.

Encourage the children to ask questions while you make the circuit, and let them use this simple circuit to light up the model made in the activity on page 56.

NB It is very important to emphasise to the children the need to take care with electricity at home and in the nursery, particularly in relation to sockets and plugs.

Talk about
Electricity, safety, battery, circuit, lights, switch on, switch off.

Follow-up
Science
● Ask the children to hold hands in a circle to make a 'circuit'. When you call a child's name, he or she lets go of the hands on either side and everybody falls down. Make it into a game rather like Ring o'Roses.
● Cut out pictures from a catalogue of household appliances that use electricity. Let the children look at machines in school that use electricity, such as the television, computer, radio and listening centre.

Lighting up

Objective
Technology: designing and making with a variety of materials.

What you need
Scrap materials, scissors, adhesive, sticky tape, paper-fasteners and clips.

What to do
Working on this activity in a group can be a worthwhile challenge for older children. It offers them the opportunity to make decisions, negotiate and plan the project together. You need to be ready to listen and help the children to put their plans into action.

Discuss with the children the buildings and vehicles that use lights, and what the lights are used for. Encourage the children to suggest buildings and vehicles with lights that they would like to make, and then ask them to choose one from the list.

Discuss with the children how they can make the model. Encourage them to look for possible materials and fasteners. It is important to let the children try out their ideas and modify them. Your role as teacher is to support and extend the children's own ideas.

Talk about
Lights. Where? Why? How? What sort of? How else?

Birthday lights

Objectives
Maths: using number, time and fractions. Science: investigating light from different sources.

What you need
A cake with candles, a knife.

What to do
Invite children who are the same age to sit together. Count the sets of children. Do they know how many are in each group? Are there more in one group than another? Match children one to one to see if there are any left over.

Make the room dark before lighting the candles on the cake. Count the candles together. Choose a child of that age, possibly one who has had a birthday recently, to blow out the candles.

Repeat the exercise with more or fewer candles until all the age groups have been covered. Slice and share the cake.

Talk about
Light, dark. How old? How many? More than, less than, the same number, share, divide, some each.

Follow-up
English
Discuss the use of lights for celebrations, including candles on birthday cakes and tree lights at Christmas. On or near to 5 November light a sparkler outside for the children to watch. This can be the starting point for discussing children's own experiences and for introducing the firework safety code.

Science
Discuss with the children the danger of lighting matches.

Shadows

Objective
Science: observing light and shadow.

What you need
A sunny day.

What to do
On a sunny day, take the children outside to look at the shadows made by different objects, such as fencing, trees and playground equipment.

Look at the sizes and shapes of the shadows. Can the children say whether they are long or short? Where is the sun? Make sure that children know not to look directly at the sun.

Ask the children to look for their own shadows. Can they make their shadows disappear? Invite them to stand in the shade of a tree or a building, which will hide their shadows.

Suggest that they play shadow tig, trying to stand on someone else's shadow.

Talk about
Sun, shadow, shade, longer than, shorter than.

Shadow stick

Objective
Science: charting the movement of the sun across the sky.

What you need
A sunny day, a stick, a bucket of sand, some chalk.

What to do
Outside in the playground, wedge a stick securely in a bucket of sand on the play area. Can the children see the shadow of the stick? Where is the sun? Draw the shadow of the stick in coloured chalk on the play area.

Ask the children to look at the shadow later to see whether there is any change. Draw the new position of the shadow. Repeat the exercise at intervals throughout the day.

Talk about
Sun, shadow, position, time, at first, later, then, at milk time, at lunch time, at home time.

Follow-up
Science
Tape a large piece of dark paper, such as black sugar paper, to the play area and mark the movement of the stick's shadow on the paper. Then the paper can be taken into the nursery for discussion.

Silhouettes

Objective
Science: investigating light and shadow.

What you need
A strong lamp or a slide projector, a backcloth such as a large piece of white paper, coloured chalk or felt-tipped pen, paper.

What to do
Invite a child to stand in front of the lamp so that a shadow of his head appears on the backcloth.

Draw round the shadow with chalk and cut the shape out. Individual facial features are more prominent when the head is in profile, but it is useful to make silhouettes from different angles and compare viewpoints.

Mount and display the silhouettes, inviting children to guess whose they are.

Talk about

Light, shadow, silhouette, features of the face and head.

Follow-up
English

Help the children to chalk or write their names on the captions for their silhouettes.

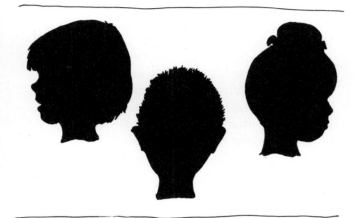

Shadow puppets

Objective

English: listening to a story.

What you need

A strong lamp or slide projector, a backcloth such as a large sheet of white paper, thick card, scissors.

What to do

Decide on a story to tell. It is most effective if the story has a number of very different characters that can readily be identified, as in the story of the little red hen, where the key characters are a hen, a cat, a dog and a rat.

Using the card, cut out the shapes of the characters and mount them on strips of card. Any key objects in the story can also be cut out, for example, the windmill and the loaf of bread.

Relate the story with the help of the cut-out characters by holding them in front of the lamp — or on the overhead projector so that their shadows appear on the backcloth.

It is also possible to make shadows with your hands to represent the characters, but this can often prove difficult to sustain.

Talk about

Puppets, shadows, shapes, story conventions, the beginning of the story, the end of the story, what happens next, and then.

Follow-up
Technology

Invite the children to design and make their own puppet or shape to show on the screen.

Let's look for black and white

Objective
Maths: sorting objects and matching for colour.

What you need
A selection of commonly-found items that are black or white, black and white paper, pencils, scissors, black and white paint, white chalk, charcoal.

What to do
Black and white items can make an effective contrast when displayed together. Include a variety of seasonal objects such as gloves, scarves, jumpers and boots.

Encourage the children to use black and white paper for making silhouettes of familiar classroom objects. They can do this by drawing round the objects and cutting them out. Mount these silhouettes on contrasting paper.

Give the children the opportunity to use white paint and chalk on black paper. Charcoal and black paint can be used on white paper. Offer children black and white paint and a choice of black or white paper. They can observe the different effects of the various combinations.

Talk about
Black, white, object names.

Follow-up
Science
Place the colour frames described in the next activity on a table, so that children can observe how colour changes.

Seeing red

Objective
Science: investigating light and colour.

What you need
Cardboard frames made from cereal or other boxes, coloured and clear acetate film, sticky tape.

What to do
Secure a sheet of acetate film to each frame with sticky tape. Invite the children to look through the sheets to see how the colour of familiar items changes.

Put together two colours such as red and yellow. What colour can the children see now? What other colours can they make using the coloured sheets? What happens when they look through the clear film?

Talk about
Light, colour names, transparent.

Follow-up
Science
Cover with coloured film some of the nursery windows which are at child height, so that the children can observe the changes in colour of various objects outside. The primary colours of light are green, red and blue.

Colour glasses

Objective
Science: looking at colour and light.

What you need
Cardboard rolls, coloured and clear acetate film, sticky tape.

What to do
Make 'colour glasses' from cardboard rolls which have coloured film taped over one end. Invite a child to choose pieces of film of one or more colours. Wrap the film over one end of the tube and secure it with sticky tape.

Two or more tubes covered with different coloured film can be fastened together. Get the children to look through the tubes. What colour do they see? Let them observe the changes in colour of familiar objects. The tubes can be easily carried about by young children and can be used for looking at colours outside.

Talk about
Colour names, light.

I spy

Objective
Science: observing colour.

What to do
Play 'I spy' using colour clues such as, 'I spy something red'. Give the children time to look for red objects around them, and then give further colour clues, for example, 'It is red with blue buttons', until the item is named.

As children become adept at identifying primary colours, introduce shades such as pale blue, as well as colours such as turquoise and beige.

Talk about
Colour and object names.

Mixing colours

Objective
Science: using colour.

What you need
Powder paint of different colours, small tubs, a water pot, a piece of sponge in a plastic container, paintbrushes, paper, a palette.

What to do
Put small samples of different powder paints in individual tubs.

Encourage the children to mix colours on the palette. Let them watch how the colour changes. Help them to make colours lighter and darker.

The children could then mix primary colours, yellow, red and blue, in different combinations, for example, red and blue to make purple. What other colours can they make?

It is useful to get children into a 'water, sponge, paint' routine with their brushes to avoid getting too much water in the powder paint tubs.

Initially, children enjoy simply watching the colours change on the palette. Later, they may want to try mixing their paints on paper. With experience, they will mix colours to paint a picture.

Talk about
Colour names and shades.

Follow-up
Science
Take the children for a colour walk, looking for colours in nature and the man-made environment.

Keeping warm

Chapter five

As days grow colder, gloves, hats and scarves become part of children's daily wardrobe. Children can investigate materials, including those that keep them warm. Sewing provides the opportunity for designing and making simple clothes and experimenting with appliqué.

When it is warm indoors and cold outside, the idea of temperature can be explored, and the effects of cooling and heating substances observed. Snowy days bring a special thrill to outdoor play, and a new substance to take inside to investigate. Looking for prints in the snow turns our attention to the hungry birds, and making a bird cake encourages children to observe and care for wildlife.

Warm or cold?

Objective
Science: exploring temperature.

What you need
A water tray, warm and cold water.

What to do
Fill the water tray with warm water. Discuss with the children how it feels. Later, let them feel the water again. Do they think it is still warm, or is it cold?

On another occasion, put some cold water in the water tray. How can the children make the water warm? Ask them to add some warm water, a little at a time. How many jugfuls did they need to add before the water felt warmer? Discuss comparative temperature, for example, a little warmer, a lot warmer. Try the reverse, starting with a little colder.

NB At no time should children be exposed to very hot or cold temperatures.

Talk about
Temperature, feels warm, warmer, cold, colder.

Chocolate crispies

Objectives
Maths: measuring with non-standard units.
Science: observing changes brought about by heating and cooling.

What you need
Six teacups of puffed rice cereal, 225g block of cooking chocolate, a saucepan, a wooden spoon, cake cases, a bowl, a cooker, a fridge.

What to do
Let the children help with this activity as much as possible.

Measure the cereal and put it in a bowl. Break up the chocolate, pointing out to the children its solid texture. Melt the chocolate in the saucepan on a low heat. Observe and discuss how the chocolate changes from solid to liquid.

When it has melted, add the chocolate to the cereal and stir until the cereal is covered in chocolate. Spoon some of the mixture into each cake case.

Place the crispies in the fridge. Ask the children to predict what will happen to the mixture.

When the chocolate has solidified, let the children taste the results.

Talk about
Measures: How much? A cupful, solid, liquid, melt, solidify.

Follow-up
Science
Make a jelly, to give the children further experience of heating and cooling a substance which changes from solid to liquid.

Snowy days

Objective
Maths: exploring shapes.

What you need
A snowy day.

What to do
Wrap the children up warmly and take them outside to look for prints in the snow. There may be prints left by birds, dogs and humans.

Ask the children to look closely at the patterns and shapes, and let them make some more prints. Compare the large adult footprints with the smaller ones made by the children. Compare the patterns on the soles of shoes with those left in the snow.

Let the children make shapes with the snow by rolling it into a ball, or by patting a pile of snow with their hands. Encourage them to make a snow sculpture. Their snow people and animals may be similar in shape to their drawings, that is, a round shape with twigs sticking out from all sides for legs, arms and ears, with eyes and a mouth in the centre.

Talk about
Snow, prints, shapes, patterns.

Follow-up
English
Encourage the children to use twigs to write their names and draw pictures in the snow.
Science
With the children, observe and discuss the wildlife and trees in the snowy conditions.

Snowflakes

Objective
Maths: looking at pattern and shape.

What you need
White paint, black paper, paintbrushes, newspaper, cotton reels, a plastic doily, white crêpe and tissue paper, scissors, cotton.

What to do
Encourage the children to print snowflakes for a frieze by dipping screwed-up newspaper or cotton reels into white paint. They could also paint over a plastic doily or cut holes in white paper to make larger snowflake mobiles.

Talk about
What sort of a pattern? What shape?

Melting snow

Objective
Science: observing the effects of heat.

What you need
Snow (or ice from the freezer), four small plastic tubs.

What to do
Divide the snow into four equal amounts and place some in each container. Place one tub near a radiator, one outside, one in the fridge and one on the discovery table.

Ask the children to predict what might happen. Let them watch closely how the snow melts in the warm room.

Later, bring all the containers together and compare the results. Can the children guess which snow melted first? Which snow has not melted? What made the snow melt? What makes the snow outside melt? Listen carefully to the children's attempts to reason and predict.

Talk about
Snow, warm, melt, liquid.

Follow-up
Science
● Let the children compare the same amount of snow in solid and liquid states. They should consider texture, colour, temperature and quantity.
● Encourage the children to hypothesise, for example, if we want to keep something cold or hot, where can we put it?

Follow-up
Science
During outside play, ask the children to watch how birds use their wings and feathers for flying. Let them look for birds with ruffled feathers. Do the children know why it is that birds ruffle their feathers?

Let's meet a bird

Objective
Science: observing the variety of life.

What you need
A pet bird in its cage.

What to do
Arrange for a pet bird and its owner to visit the nursery. Leave the bird in its cage on the discovery table to encourage the children to look closely at its features and habits.

Point to the bird's feathers. Do the children know what colours they are? Can they see any small fluffy feathers? Where are they?

Invite the owner to bring along the bird's food and any equipment needed to look after it. Ask the children if they know what the bird eats. Where does it sleep? How does it move? What does it use its claws for?

Talk about
Birds, species, naming the parts of a bird, claw, beak, wings.

Feathers

Objectives
Maths: looking at shape and pattern.
Science: using feathers for keeping warm.

What you need
A collection of feathers from different birds, a magnifying glass.

What to do
Discuss with the children the birds that can be seen outside the nursery in cold weather. Do they know how the birds keep warm? Show the feathers to the children. With the children's help, sort out the small fluffy feathers that lie close to the bird's body from the longer, stiffer ones.

Let the children look closely at a feather using the magnifying glass. Identify and discuss its parts. Now let them look at the feather with the magnifying glass after running a finger up and then down the barbs.

Talk about
Feathers, colour, texture, shape, parts.

Follow-up
Maths
Let the children print using feathers of different sizes. Point out to them the patterns and shapes.
Science
Ask the children to look closely at the colours of a feather. Let them mix powder paints to give these colours.

Feeding the birds

Objectives
Science: looking after wildlife and observing the effects of heat on materials.

What you need
Chopped nuts (not roasted or salted), seeds (eg sunflower), bread, cheese, bacon scraps, lard to bind the dry ingredients, a spoon, a coconut broken into two, a saucepan, a cooker, a fridge, string.

What to do
Let the children help as much as possible in making a bird cake.

Melt the lard in the saucepan over a low heat. Add the nuts, seeds and scraps and mix together.

Pour the mixture into the coconut halves. Cool the mixture in the fridge.

Make two holes in each coconut shell and thread with string. Hang the coconuts full of bird cake by the string from a tree or bush, out of the way of predators.

If possible, hang the coconut halves within sight of the nursery windows, so

that the children can watch birds feed when the playground is quiet. It is unlikely that birds will feed when the children are outside. However, they will be able to see how the bird cake gets smaller, showing that birds have been feeding in their absence.

Talk about
The food birds eat, nuts, seed, fruit, melting and cooling.

Four scarlet berries

Objective
Maths: introducing number.

What to do
Encourage the children to use the fingers on one hand to represent the berries and to shape the other hand like a bird's beak. Count the berries before starting the rhyme with the children. Introduce the idea of 'none'.

Four scarlet berries
Left on the tree.
'Thanks', said the blackbird,
'These will do for me.'
He ate numbers one and two,
And then ate number three;
When he'd eaten number four,
There was none to see.

Mary Vivian

Let's meet a rabbit

Objective
Science: observing how fur keeps animals warm.

What you need
A pet rabbit.

What to do
Arrange for a pet rabbit to visit the nursery. Make some suitable accommodation for the rabbit so that the children can observe its features and habits. Do the children know what it eats? Where does it sleep? How does it keep warm? How does it move?

Talk about
Rabbits, naming parts, ears, whiskers, tail.

Follow-up
English
Ask the children to talk about their pets. What types do they have? Do their pets have fur or feathers to keep them warm?

Keeping warm

Objective
Science: looking at types and uses of fabrics.

What you need
Four small plastic soft drinks bottles with tight-fitting lids, a fur-lined hat or mitten, a knitted mitten, a thin summer hat or sock, sticky tape, warm water.

What to do
Put some warm water in each bottle. Do not use very hot water as the children will hold the bottles. Tightly close the lids and seal them with sticky tape to avoid spillage. Cover one bottle with a fur-lined mitten or hat, one with a knitted mitten, one with a thin hat or sock, and leave the other exposed.

Return to the bottles later. Let the children feel how warm they are. Do they know which is the warmest and which is the coldest? Can they say which clothes keep us warm? What fabrics are these made from?

Talk about
How warm? Warm, cold, warmest, coldest, fabric names and textures.

Follow-up
Science
• Gather together a selection of children's scarves, coats, hats and gloves. Do the children know what the garments are made from? How do we keep warm?
• Cover a bottle of warm water with foil to provide experience of other insulating materials.

Appliqué

Objective
Science: investigating types of materials.

What you need
A large table-sized piece of hessian or loosely woven cloth, fabric of different types, for example, fur, cotton, netting and acrylic.

What to do
Place the hessian on a table top. Encourage a group of children to choose, cut, position and sew on their own fabric pieces. Tip: Knot the thread at the needle end to prevent it from slipping out with every stich.

Talk about
Fabric names, colours, texture and pattern.

Clothes

Objectives
Maths: looking at pattern and shape.
Science: investigating mirrors and reflection.

What you need
A full-length mirror, preferably free-standing, with unbreakable glass, an easel, paints, paintbrushes, paper.

What to do
Place the mirror by the easel. Ask each child in turn to look in the mirror at the clothes they are wearing and to talk about the patterns and shapes. Do they know the colours of the clothes? Encourage the children to paint a picture of themselves in the clothes they are wearing.

Talk about
Clothes, naming items, their colour, shape, pattern and texture.

Let's meet a knitter

Objective
Science: using wool for making clothes.

What you need
A keen knitter, balls of wool, knitting needles.

What to do
Invite a parent or grandparent who can knit to show the children how a garment is knitted. Show the children garments which have been knitted previously, and let them look at their size, shape and colour.

A garment for the home corner baby can be knitted very quickly. Ask the children to choose an article of clothing they would like to have made, and to select the colour. They can then watch the process from the ball of wool to the finished garment.

Talk about
Wool, thread, needles, stitches, rows, names of garments.

Making clothes

Objectives
Maths: measuring with non-standard units.
Technology: designing and making.

What you need
Fabrics, for example, old curtains, needles, threads, masking tape, string, paper, scissors.

What to do
Invite each child to design and make an item of clothing for a favourite toy.

Encourage the children to choose their own fabrics and help them to measure using non-standard units, such as string or paper strips torn or cut to size. The garment can be sewn or fastened together with masking tape.

Talk about
What does the toy need? What can we use? How can we measure it? Does it fit? How shall we join it?

Follow-up
Technology
Encourage the children to watch and participate when clothes for the role-play area are being made, so that they can see why accurate measurement is needed.

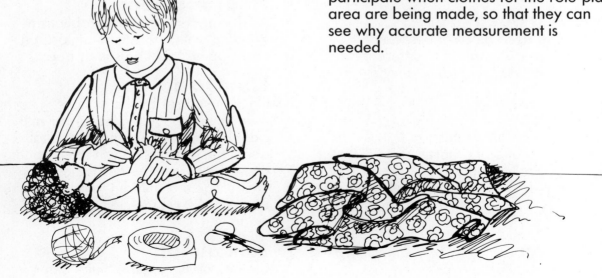

Let's look for fasteners

Objective
Technology: investigating methods of attaching materials.

What you need
Items of children's clothing with a variety of fastenings.

What to do
Display a collection of children's clothes, possibly from the spare clothes box, which have different fasteners, for example, buttons, poppers, zips, hooks and eyes, laces, buckles, toggles, belts and velcro.

Encourage the children to explore the fasteners, attempting to put them together and take them apart. Invite them to look for fasteners on their own clothes. Learning to use fasteners helps to develop the skills required for changing their own clothes. Encourage children to help each other.

Talk about
Fasteners, their names, methods of attachment and parts.

Sorting gloves

Objective
Maths: sorting and matching for shape, colour and pattern.

What you need
Several pairs of gloves.

What to do
This activity is useful on days when the radiators are covered with drying gloves that need to be sorted and returned to their owners.

Show the children a glove, and discuss its colour, pattern, type and fabric. Invite the children to search for one that matches. Repeat the exercise until, with luck, each glove finds its partner.

Talk about
Match, not match, the same, different, colour and texture names.

Follow-up
Maths
With a small number of gloves, encourage the children to think about probability. Ask them how many gloves they think will need to be pulled out of the box before they have a pair.

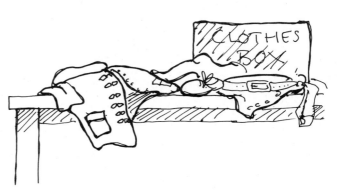

Let's look for soft and hard

Objective
Science: sorting types of material into broad categories.

What you need
A variety of seasonal items which are hard or soft.

What to do
Invite the children to search in the nursery for soft and hard items. Seasonal soft items may include scarves, hats, jumpers, and gloves. Hard items may include a shovel and twigs. Other items related to the topics previously covered are containers, threads, string and soft toys.

Talk about
Hard and soft materials, their texture and function, harder than, softer than.

Toys

Chapter six

As Christmas approaches, toys are displayed in the shops and on television. Moving toys can provide a starting point for investigating forces and energy, and children can design and make their own toys that move.

Children will see toys wrapped and sent through the post as Christmas presents, and sometimes they can help with this at home. Creating a classroom post office gives many opportunities for maths and literacy activities, and leads to role-play that stimulates children's reading and writing behaviour.

Let's discover toys that move

Objective
Science and technology: observing that toys move in different ways.

What you need
A selection of toys that move, such as vehicles, dolls with moving arms and legs, a spinning top, a ball, battery-driven toys, water puzzles, a rocking toy.

What to do
Let the children have a close look at the toys, and then find out what they have noticed.

Do they know how the toy moves? Does it spin, roll or bounce? How can we make it move? Do we have to push it or switch it on? Does the toy move forwards, backwards, turn in circles or go up and down?

Talk about
Moving, spin, roll, bounce, direction, forwards, backwards, up, down, sideways.

Follow-up
Maths
Ask the children to use their bodies to move in different ways: walk, slide, rock, crawl and roll. Let them try moving in different directions: backwards, forwards, sideways, to the left and right.

Science
● During outdoor play, let the children experiment with toys that move. Do they have to push, pull, rock or pedal them? Let them examine the see-saw, rocking boat, swing, trolley and pram. How do they move?

● Use hardboard sheets and smooth planks to make slopes. Place different shaped bricks and packaging on the ramps, for example, cuboids and cylinders. Ask the children to describe and name the shapes that roll down the slopes.

76

Making a toy that moves

Objective
Technology: designing and making a toy that moves.

What you need
Scrap materials, for example, boxes, card, paper, fabric, adhesive, masking tape, paper-clips, paper-fasteners.

What to do
Encourage the children to design and make a toy that moves. This may take the simplest form.
• Children could use an egg box to make a crocodile that opens and closes its mouth.
• They could bend or cut a flexible material, for example, cutting a flap to make a door that opens and closes in a cereal-box house.

• A fastener could be used for the same effect, for example, putting tape along one side of a piece of card to make a flap for an animal's ears or a bird's wings.
• Paper-fasteners are useful for moving parts such as arms and legs, but you will have to fix them on. Fasten thick card circles on to the sides of simple box vehicles to make wheels that roll. Cut circles of different sizes so that children can match wheels for size, or use two large and two small ones to make a tractor.

Talk about
How can we make it move? What can we use? What else can we try?

Rolling prints

Objective
Maths: observing pattern and shape.

What you need
Some plastic washable vehicles, a ball, cylinders, bricks, a tray, paper, paints.

What to do
Place a sheet of paper at the bottom of the tray.

Ask the children to dip the ball or vehicle wheels in the paint and roll them along the paper in the tray. They can then try to do the same with the cylinders and bricks.

Talk about
Rolls, does not roll, slides, sphere, circle, parallel.

Follow-up
Maths
Let the children have a go at printing with bicycle and other wheels on long sheets of wallpaper.

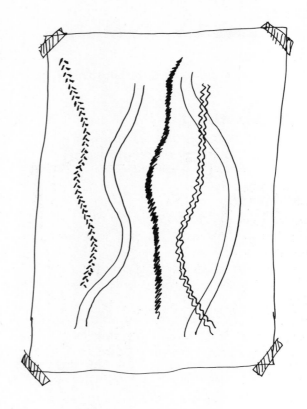

Painting with two brushes

Objective
Maths: exploring linear tracks.

What you need
Two paintbrushes, a piece of wood, masking tape, paper, paint.

What to do
Place the piece of wood between the brushes and bind them together with masking tape. This will separate the strokes made by the two brushes.

When the children are using the brushes, discuss the path of the lines as the brushes turn and twist over the paper.

Talk about
Lines, same distance apart, meet, parallel, one line, turn, same direction.

Follow-up
Maths
Let the children dip some combs with different sized teeth in paint, and then pull the combs over a sheet of paper.

Toy catalogue

Objective
Maths: introducing number notation.

What you need
A clipboard, paper, pencil, a toy catalogue, adhesive.

What to do
Invite some of the children to cut out a picture of their favourite toy from a catalogue. Stick the pictures down one side of a piece of paper. One child should then ask another which is her favourite toy. The child can then make a mark or tally to indicate the preference next to the picture. Several children can be asked and the results recorded in the same way. The totals can then be counted.

Children can make their own tally system. Some use straight lines, others use numerals, while some invent their own system.

Talk about
How many? Number names, adding on one, one more.

What have I got in my toy shop today?

Objective
English: listening and responding to rhyme.

What to do
With the children, sing the following rhyme to the tune of 'Here we go round the mulberry bush':

What have I got in my toy shop today,
Toy shop today, toy shop today:
What have I got in my toy shop today?
Who [or child's name] can tell me?

You should then describe a toy in words and keep giving clues until one of the children guesses it correctly. Do the same again with another toy.

Guess the toy

Objective
Science: exploring and developing the sense of touch.

What you need
A large fabric bag with a draw-string opening, a selection of toys.

What to do
When the children are not looking, put a toy in the bag. Then ask one of them to feel inside the bag and guess what the toy is.

When the children are familiar with the game they can choose toys for their friends to guess.

Talk about
What does it feel like? Soft, hard, smooth, rough.

A toy adventure

Objective
English: telling a story.

What you need
A toy, paper, a stapler, pencils, crayons.

What to do
Tell the children a story which features a well-loved nursery toy. Use the toy, which may be a doll, soft toy or vehicle, as a prop when you tell the story. Children generally enjoy listening to such stories, especially when they include details of other familiar nursery places, people and events.

Involve the children in creating the story. Ask for their ideas and incorporate them into the narrative. Later, write the story in book form. Ask the children to draw pictures to illustrate it. Leave it in the book corner to encourage reading behaviour.

Talk about
Telling a story. What happened next? Who was there? What did they do?

Follow-up
Technology
Ask the children how to bind the book. This is an exercise in problem-solving. Offer suggestions, if necessary, such as sewing or using a binder. Listen to the children's ideas, which will probably include sticky tape, paper-clips and considerable ingenuity!

Making a puppet

Objective
Technology: designing, making and problem-solving with a variety of materials.

What you need
Scrap materials, for example, paper bags, cardboard rolls and socks, an assortment of fabrics, bottle tops, shredded paper, paper-clips, sticky tape, thread, crayons.

What to do
Invite the children to make a hand puppet. Give them a variety of materials to use. Listen to their ideas and help them to achieve their goal. Offer suggestions if necessary, such as using a decorated paper bag, a sock or a cardboard roll for the main body of the puppet.

Talk about
How? What can we use? How can we fasten it? What sort of . . .?

Follow-up
English
Have a puppet show, using the puppets to tell a story.

Let's visit a post office

Objectives
English: using literacy.
Maths: covering a shape and weighing.

What you need
Some toys or books in good condition, a large box, wrapping paper, sticky tape, a letter and a card made by the children themselves.

What to do
Arrange to visit a post office with the children. Before the visit, collect some toys or books to send to a hospital. The children can make a card to accompany it (see page 87). Find a box that fits the toys. Let the children help you to wrap up the parcel, label it and write the address. They can then hold it to see how heavy it is.

Encourage the children to write a letter to another nursery, telling them about their favourite toy or activity. This letter may well take the form of pictures and mark-making.

At the post office, let the children watch as the package is weighed and the necessary stamps bought. Buy a stamp for the letter and ask one of the children to post it in the post-box. If possible, try to arrange the visit to coincide with the emptying of the post-box.

Many post offices sell toys and gifts as well as wrapping paper, labels and string. Discuss the toys, gifts and cards on sale. Let the children look closely at the wrapping paper, which often has recurring patterns. Read to the children some of the notices and forms for the customers' use.

Talk about
Sending gifts and cards, stamps, address, postcode.

Let's make a post office

Objective
English: encouraging literacy in role-play.

What you need
Forms, labels, stickers, posters from a post office, a selection of toys, rolls of wallpaper for wrapping gifts, paper, pencils, crayons, used envelopes, stamps cut with pinking shears from sticky-back paper, a post box made from a painted cardboard box with a slit, a date stamp or a picture stamp, used stamps, pretend money, a cap and sack for the postman.

What to do
Convert the home corner or role-play area into a post office that also sells toys and cards. This will give the children an opportunity to buy and wrap gifts, as well as post them.

Talk about
Sending letters, writing, reading, fits, not enough, more.

Follow-up
English
Encourage the children to improve their writing skills as they fill in order forms and cards. Make notices for the post office and read them with the children.
Maths
Encouraging the children to wrap presents involves them in thinking about shape and area.

Let's meet the postman

Objectives
English: using literacy.
Maths: observing shape and size.

What you need
A visit from the local postman or -woman.

What to do
Arrange for the postman or -woman to come into the nursery when the post is delivered.

Ask the children to look at the uniform. Do they know how the postman arrives at school? By van, bicycle or on foot? Where are the letters and packages kept? Ask them how the postman knows where to deliver them. Let them look at the letters and packets for school. How many are there? What size and shape are they? Who are they for? It may be possible to open one of the school's letters with the children and discuss its contents.

Talk about
Post, the uses of writing and reading, size, shape and weight of packets and letters.

Follow-up
Technology
Take the children to make a telephone call from a local call box to school, to show them another way of sending a message. Alternatively, use the school telephone to contact someone who is willing to talk with the children.

Card for a special occasion

Objective
English: encouraging mark-making.

What you need
Card and paper of different colours, crayons, pencils, an adhesive stick.

What to do
Encourage each child to draw a picture of her own choice. Mount the picture on paper of another colour. Stick this on to a piece of card folded in half. Write the child's message inside the card, and encourage the child to write her own name below the message.

The result will be a card that reflects the individual child and is treasured by her family. It is also a useful idea for celebrating different festivals.

Talk about
Writing, message. What does it say?

Let's look for plastic

Objective
Science: investigating types and uses of materials.

What you need
A variety of items made from plastic.

What to do
Ask the children to collect a selection of articles made from plastic, starting with toys. Other seasonal items include Christmas decorations, rain hoods and ice-scrapers.

Talk about
Plastic, its texture, colours, durability.

Follow-up
Science
Introduce the idea of materials that decompose and those that do not. Let the children help you to bury a small plastic object and some tissue paper in wet soil in a bucket. After a while, look at the tissue and look at the plastic. Can the children see what has happened to the tissue? Has the plastic changed? Do they know how else we can use paper and plastic?

Topic planning
Chapter seven

The seasons provide opportunities for topics that are very broad in scope. Relevant activities can take place throughout the nursery, with sand, water, construction kits, the writing centre and all the other indoor equipment, as well as outdoor and role-play. At the same time, well-planned seasonal topics can cater for all areas of the curriculum, providing children with experience in English, maths, science and technology.

Topics as starting points

Teachers can plan a topic that will enrich the children's experience of everyday nursery activities and enhance their awareness of the world around them. Seasonal topics can easily be adapted to cater for children's individual interests, and they provide plenty of stimulus for related activities. Topics should always be regarded as a way of awakening children's own interests. It is these interests, which often bring a new slant to the familiar, that determine the course of the topic.

Involving parents

Topic work provides an opportunity for parents to become involved in their child's education, as they discuss and extend their child's experiences at home. Seasonal topics certainly offer an accessible source of material for discussion at home, and this material can also be brought in for investigation at school. In this way learning at home and at school takes place in harmony.

Informing parents

Parents need to be informed of the term's topic. One way of doing this is to use a display board near the cloakroom as a parent's noticeboard. Pin up the following pieces of information for parents to read:
● the topic planning sheet (pages 92 and 94–95) in an easy-to-read form;
● details of the investigation tables, so that parents and children can bring in objects for discussion in school;
● requests for visitors, such as someone who can knit, to show their work and sit with the children.

Information for parents can also bring unexpected bonuses in the form of equipment for the role-play area.

Planning topic work

- First of all, have a brainstorming session that involves everyone who will be working with the children. This will alert all the staff to potential activities, and ensure a co-ordinated approach.
- Write down every idea, even those that seem irrelevant; they may spark off something worthwhile later.
- Organise the ideas to ensure that there is breadth and balance in the curriculum. It may be helpful to plan initially in curriculum areas and then convert this into an action plan for the nursery (see page 92). The action plan gives a clearer idea of resources and structuring required.
- Remember that plans are a springboard to encourage children's own ideas. Be prepared to modify, change and even ignore aspects of them in order to extend children's own developing interests.

The topic sheet

Page 92 shows an example of a filled-in initial planning sheet. Photocopiable pages 94 and 95 provide blank master-sheets for you to fill in. The separate sections of the chart act as a checklist to ensure that each area of the nursery is considered at the planning stage. When the boxes are filled in with activities and page numbers they provide an overview of the implementation of the topic. There is also room in the boxes to give an idea of the additional resources required.

The subject areas for the individual activities can be identified according to NCC guidelines: En for English, Ma for maths, Sc for science and Te for technology. However, the identification of subject areas will be based on the teacher's intention for the activity. A child may respond to the activity in a way not anticipated and yet equally valid. The activities undertaken will be a source of imaginative and physical play, as well as a means of social and emotional development. This needs to be recognised by staff in their response to children's play. Topic work gives the opportunity to offer additional experiences and activities to children to enhance their play, stimulate their curiosity and widen their horizons.

Topic - Autumn. leaves, fruit and vegetables

Role-play
1) Supermarket (P.30) - real potatoes and balance, shopping bag, Money, purse, till.
2) Food packages (empty) and cans.
3) Pad and pencil for shopping lists and messages.
4) Supermarket layouts - recipes etc.

Writing centre
1) Pictorial recipe for apple pie (P.39).
2) Survey of favourite fruit (P.36).
3) Captions and labels for display and investigation tables. Children's mark making and teacher as scribe.
4) Shopping lists and phone messages.

Book corner
1) Way rhyme for 'Autumn leaves' (P.18)
2) Information books about leaves, fruit and vegetables.
3) Felt board figures and props from 'The Enormous Turnip' to encourage storytelling (P.35).

Visits
1) Park - trees and leaves (P.11).
2) Supermarket - fruit and vegetables, fresh, frozen, canned, preserved.

Paint
1) Printing with leaves, twigs and cones (P.14).
2) Vegetable prints (P.32)
3) Colour mixing - shades of orange and brown (P.62).

Natural materials

Clay
Impressions with twigs, leaves, conkers, cones and acorns (P.23).

Dough
Modelling dough to make 'food' for role-play (PP.45 and 46).

Sand
Twigs for mark-making. Cones, conkers and leaves for impressions and imaginative play.

Water
Leaves, twigs, cones, potato and apple for floating and sinking.

Visitors
Refuse collector: leaf litter, waste paper (P.21).

Music and movement
1) Listening to and using wooden instruments (P.28).
2) Using parts of a tree (acorns, cones, bark) in shakers (P.28).
3) Movement - the story of the enormous turnip (P.35).

Food
1) Leaves we eat (P.21): coleslaw (P.22); herbs (P.22).
2) Vegetables (PP.31 and 33); Soup (P.34); carrot cake (P.34).
3) Fruit (P.31): fruit juice (P.37); apple pie (P.39); fruit salad (P.36).

Construction

Equipment
using wooden blocks, noting texture and shapes. Investigating how blocks fit together - balance and tessellation (P.28).

Scrap materials
1) Autumn collage - twigs, leaves, grasses (P.23).
2) Sewing autumn leaves (P.16).
3) Leaf, bark and tree ring rubbing (P.15).
4) Designing and making with wood off-cuts and cones (P.28).

Outdoor
1) Looking for seasonal changes (P.11).
2) Looking at trees and the use of wood (P.28).
3) Measuring tree trunks (P.27).
4) Planting bulbs (P.25).

Investigation tables
1) Leaves (P.12): box of leaves (P.17); falling leaves (P.17); growing a tree from a seed (P.37).
2) Wood (P.28): toys, household equipment: rough, smooth, polished; wood to sand; old wooden artefacts.

Other

92

Book list

Leaves, fruit and vegetables

Each Peach Pear Plum, Janet and Allan Ahlberg (Picture Lions).
Avocado Baby, John Burningham (Picture Lions).
The Shopping Basket, John Burningham (Picture Lions).
Going Shopping, Sarah Garland (Picture Puffin).
Spot's First Walk, Eric Hill (Picture Puffin).
Rosie's Walk, Pat Hutchins (Picture Puffin).
Everybody said No, Sheila Lavelle (A & C Black).
Meg's Veg, Helen Nichol and Jan Pienkowski (Picture Puffin).
The Great Big Enormous Turnip, Alexei Tolstoy and Helen Oxenbury (Piccolo).

Bread

The Little Red Hen, Paul Galdone (World's Work).
Benny bakes a cake, Eve Rice (Bodley Head).

Day and night

Burglar Bill, Janet and Allan Ahlberg (Picture Lions).
Funnybones, Janet and Allan Ahlberg (Picture Lions).
I want to see the moon, Louis Baum (Magnet).
Colours, Shirley Hughes (Walker).
Goodnight Owl, Pat Hutchins (Picture Puffin).
Nandy's Bedtime, Errol Lloyd (Bodley Head).
Peace at Last, Jill Murphy (Picturemac).
Moonlight, Jan Ormerod (Picture Puffin).
Sunshine, Jan Ormerod (Picture Puffin).

Tom and Pippo's Day, Helen Oxenbury (Walker).
Tom and Pippo see the Moon, Helen Oxenbury (Walker).
Goodnight, Goodnight, Eve Rice (Picture Puffin).

Keeping warm

Sally-Ann in the Snow, Petronella Breinburg (Bodley Head).
The Snowman, Raymond Briggs (Picture Puffin).
Borka, John Burningham (Jonathan Cape).
New Clothes for Alex, Mary Dickson (Hippo).
Alfie's Feet, Shirley Hughes (Picture Lions).
Two Shoes New Shoes, Shirley Hughes (Walker).
The snowy day, Ezra Jack Keats (Picture Puffin).
Tom and Pippo go for a walk, Helen Oxenbury (Walker).
How do I put it on?, Shigeo Watanabe (Picture Puffin).

Toys

The Jolly Postman, Janet and Allan Ahlberg (Heinemann).
Sally-Ann's Skateboard, Petronella Breinburg (Bodley Head).
Sean's Red Bike, Petronella Breinburg (Bodley Head).
Dear Zoo, Rod Campbell (Picture Puffin).
Postman Pat, various titles, John Cunliffe (Hippo).
Dogger, Shirley Hughes (Picture Lions).
Lotta's Bike, Astrid Lindgren (Magnet).
Are you there, bear?, Ron Maris (Picture Puffin).

Topic planning sheet

Role-play	Paint
Writing centre	**Natural materials** Clay Dough Sand
Book corner	
Visits	**Visitors**

Food

Music and movement

Construction

Equipment

Scrap materials

Outdoor

Investigation tables

Other